THE MAGA MOVEMENT

RESHAPING AMERICA'S POLITICAL LANDSCAPE

THE MAGA MOVEMENT

RESHAPING AMERICA'S POLITICAL LANDSCAPE

Mary Cortez

LERNER PUBLICATIONS ◆ MINNEAPOLIS

Lerner Publications Company
An imprint of Lerner Publishing Group, Inc.
241 First Avenue North
Minneapolis, MN 55401 USA

For reading levels and more information, look up this title at www.lernerbooks.com.

Main body text set in ITC Garamond Std Book.
Typeface provided by Adobe Systems.

Library of Congress Cataloging-in-Publication Data

Names: Cortez, Mary author
Title: The MAGA movement : reshaping America's political landscape / Mary Cortez.
Other titles: Make America Great Again movement
Description: Minneapolis : Lerner Publications, [2026] | Series: Gateway headlines | Includes bibliographical references and index. | Audience: Ages 9–14 | Audience: Grades 4–6 | Summary: "Donald Trump's 2016 presidential campaign introduced the slogan Make America Great Again (MAGA) to a new generation of voters. But the slogan has a long history. Learn about MAGA's origins and the movement's future goals"—Provided by publisher.
Identifiers: LCCN 2025013625 (print) | LCCN 2025013626 (ebook) | ISBN 9798765690666 library binding | ISBN 9798348028664 paperback | ISBN 9798765695425 epub
Subjects: LCSH: MAGA movement—History | Political participation—United States—History—21st century
Classification: LCC JK2391.M34 C67 2026 (print) | LCC JK2391.M34 (ebook) | DDC 320.520973—dc23/eng/20250711

LC record available at https://lccn.loc.gov/2025013625
LC ebook record available at https://lccn.loc.gov/2025013626

Manufactured in the United States of America
1 - CG - 12/15/25

TABLE OF CONTENTS

Donald J. Trump (*center*) addresses a crowd of people at the US Capitol during his second presidential inauguration on January 20, 2025.

It was January 20, 2025, and Donald J. Trump had been elected the 47th president of the United States. The election had been certified fourteen days earlier, and Trump was about to take the oath of office and give an inaugural speech. Every new president since George Washington had addressed a speech to the country. Although styles and subjects differed over the years, the theme had generally been the same: unity. The inaugural speech marks the end of the campaign and the beginning of the president's role as a representative of the people—all the people.

About two hundred forty thousand people had traveled to Washington, DC, from around the world to hear the president's words. They filled the National Mall, home to the Lincoln Memorial, the Washington Monument, and other historic icons of the United States. Many people wore red Make America Great Again (MAGA) hats and waved Trump campaign flags in the air. The inauguration had been moved inside due to frigid temperatures, and only a handful of people would get a chance to watch on large screens from inside the nearby Capital One Arena. Many slept outside in the snow and woke up early to wait in a line that stretched for blocks to enter the arena. "Standing in cold weather is nothing compared to what [Trump] has given up," one supporter said.

Trump supporters wait in line outside the Capital One Arena on Inauguration Day.

In his speech, Trump spoke out against his predecessor, Joe Biden. Trump attacked the federal government, calling it corrupt. He referenced what he called a declining health care system and a failing education system. Trump vowed to solve these difficult problems. "During every single day of the Trump administration, I will, very simply, put America first," he promised. He named his Inauguration Day "Liberation Day." Trump supporters cheered as he said, "It is my hope that our recent presidential election will be remembered as the greatest and most consequential election in the history of our country." He called his advisors and political allies "American patriots" and promised he would make America great again by fixing health care, improving emergency services, and upending the education system.

Reid Beck, a supporter from North Carolina, waited out in the cold for seven hours hoping for a spot in the arena. Even though he didn't get one, he found groups of like-minded supporters. Finding people with the same beliefs was comforting. Some had been to Trump's first inauguration in 2017. Others had been in Washington, DC, on January 6, 2021—a day when Trump falsely insisted the 2020 election had been stolen.

On that day in 2021, a crowd of fifty-three thousand people had listened to Trump speak at a park about 2 miles (3.2 km) from the US Capitol where the election results were being certified. Joe Biden won the election, but Trump told the crowd that the election had been stolen and not to give up. He told them to fight. And he encouraged them to go to the Capitol. Then, he got into his vehicle and drove away.

Members of the far-right group Proud Boys gather to listen to the inauguration.

The crowd made their way to the Capitol. They fought their way inside, swarming around barriers and attacking Capitol police. Windows were broken. Officers were attacked and beaten. Members of Congress sheltered together for safety. They begged President Trump to speak to his supporters. He was the only one who could call them off. Trump had returned to the White House and sat in the dining room off the Oval Office, watching the events unfold on TV. But Trump refused to intervene. Instead, he posted messages on social media about the election being stolen.

Nine people lost their lives in connection with the riot. More than 140 police officers were injured. Eventually, 1,583 people were arrested, and 1,270 were charged for their participation in the riot. To many of Trump's supporters, the January 6 rioters were heroes, even martyrs. However, despite their efforts, security was re-established at the Capitol. The certification went ahead, and Biden was officially named president later that month.

At Trump's second inauguration in January 2025, his supporters felt enthusiastic for the future. "We have a president that actually cares about people and not just about himself and the rich elite but a president that genuinely loves America," Beck said. To him, Trump was about to make America great again.

Ronald Reagan was an actor before being elected governor of California in 1966.

MAKE AMERICA GREAT AGAIN

Ronald Reagan used the slogan Let's Make America Great Again during his presidential campaign in 1980. The country was going through economic troubles. Inflation was high, and the soaring prices meant people were struggling to buy even household basics. Nearly eight million Americans were unemployed. Few new jobs were being created.

Reagan promised his plan, called Reaganomics, would turn things around. He vowed to give corporations more tax cuts and fewer regulations. He spent less on Medicaid and Social Security, programs that provide benefits to millions of Americans, believing that the money saved would trickle down to everyday people. He also poured money into military spending. His slogan was meant to inspire Americans. And it did. He won the election in a landslide. Reagan's words—and his ideas—would find new life more than three decades later.

Reagan's second term as president ended in 1989. The next few presidents alternated between Democrats and Republicans. When Democrat Barack Obama won the office in 2008, America signaled that it was ready for a change. He became the first Black president, capturing the attention of young people and Black and Hispanic voters. Four years later, Obama won a second term by defeating Republican candidate Mitt Romney.

Obama's win was a blow to the Republican Party. Some blamed Romney for being too moderate. His middle-ground policies were even more maddening to those who identified as Tea Party members. The Tea Party was a conservative movement that had sprung up during Obama's first presidential term, partly in response to his Making Home Affordable plan. The plan launched in 2009 and committed $275 billion in government funds to help people who were struggling to pay home mortgages. Some Republicans protested. CNBC commentator Rick Santelli spoke out against the government stepping in and using taxpayer money to bail out homeowners. Inspired by the Boston Tea Party in 1773 that protested unfair taxation on tea and other issues, Santelli called for a new tea party. The name stuck, and the Tea Party movement was born.

Barack Obama (*left*) was the country's first Black president.

Tea Partiers weren't just conservatives unhappy with Democrats and moderate Republicans. They were also libertarians who believed that the government had no place in people's everyday lives. One of the Tea Party's uniting principles was birtherism, or the false belief or false claim that Obama had not been born in the US and was therefore not eligible to be president. Another was populism, the belief that the concerns of the common people should be valued over those of the elite, such as career politicians and billionaires. "Drain the swamp", also originally popularized by Reagan, became a common populist motto. Washington, DC, was built on a swamp that was drained to build the city. But to Tea Party members, "drain the swamp" meant getting rid of dishonest and corrupt politicians and the bureaucrats that supported them.

In 2010 Tea Party members organized the Tea Party Express bus tour. The tour's goal was to promote conservative Congressional candidates.

Many Tea Party members were elected to government positions as Republicans. They focused on shaking up Washington and the federal government. Tea Partiers were willing to go to extreme measures to make a point. They weren't interested in negotiating and compromising with Democrats. In 2013 Tea Party Republicans forced the government to shut down between October 1 and 17 in opposition to the Affordable Care Act, a health-care plan that had provided health insurance to many Americans since 2010. Around eight hundred thousand federal workers waited, worried about their jobs. Another 1.3 million went to work, not knowing if they would be paid. In the end, the shutdown cost the country an estimated $2 billion in lost work hours. But the Tea Party had demonstrated its power and made the voices of its members heard.

The radical change that the Tea Party advocated appealed to Trump. He had been toying with the idea of a presidential run for years. He had even considered running in 2012 before bowing out. After Romney's loss, Trump decided the time was right. He would run in 2016. Make America Great Again was officially trademarked by his campaign, Donald J. Trump for President.

America First

MAGA is Trump's main slogan. But America First is another slogan he often uses. To many, placing American interests and goals before all others makes sense. However, the slogan has a dark history. America First has historically been associated with anti-Semitic, racist, and xenophobic beliefs. After World War I (1914–1918), it was adopted by the hate group the Ku Klux Klan. Later, American newspaper publisher and politician William Randolph Hearst used it as a motto to justify staying out of World War II (1939–1945). He published flattering articles about German leader Adolf Hitler and other dictators.

In 1940 Americans from various political backgrounds formed the America First Committee. Its main message was to keep America out of foreign wars. Many of the committee members were anti-Semitic and supported fascist governments such as the Nazi Party in Germany. Modern adherents of America First policies support less intervention in the affairs of other countries and more investment in the United States. However, the slogan is still used by several anti-Semitic and white supremacist groups.

Trump speaks at an America First Policy Institute Gala at Mar-a-Lago, his luxury resort in Palm Beach, Florida, in 2024.

WHEN WAS AMERICA GREAT?

Trump made his bid for president official in 2015. In 2016 Trump campaign merchandise, including the iconic red MAGA hats, was a common sight in the United States. By early 2023, more than two million hats had been sold. Trump's son-in-law Jared Kushner claims that, at their height, the hats were bringing in $80,000 a day.

In 2016 the *New York Times* asked Trump when he thought America had been great. He cited the early twentieth century, especially when Theodore Roosevelt was president from 1901 to 1909. It was a time of military and industrial expansion. The country's population

Theodore Roosevelt is still considered to be one of the most popular presidents ever.

had nearly doubled between 1870 and 1900 due to immigration. Roosevelt ended monopolies that gave railroad and oil corporations unfair advantages. His Square Deal in 1902 negotiated the end of a coal-workers strike to ensure people had enough fuel to stay warm. Like Trump, Roosevelt used the power of the media to speak directly to the American people.

Trump also believes that the period right after World War II was a time of greatness for the United States. The economy boomed, and soldiers returned home and found jobs. People who had historically faced higher rates of unemployment–such as women, people of color, and recent immigrants–were able to find work. The middle class expanded, and more people were able to buy homes, go to college, and buy cars. The GI Bill gave veterans federal aid for education, home loans, and job training.

Despite sharing the slogan, Trump doesn't believe that Reagan enacted MAGA policies during his time in office. Reagan opened trade between the United States, Mexico, and Canada. But Trump's version of MAGA rejects globalism, the belief that people, goods, and services should move freely across borders. It rejects the idea of liberal immigration policies. Trump promised that he would focus on the United States and bring back jobs, cut taxes, and deport undocumented immigrants.

Many MAGA critics question who these policies are supposed to benefit. Some MAGA beliefs–such as ending diversity and equity programs, pushing for deportations of undocumented people, international students, and even naturalized citizens without due process, and limiting health-care choices—are seen as especially harmful to people of color, women, and immigrants. According to multiple surveys and demographic studies, including the Panel Study of the MAGA Movement by professors Christopher Sebastian Parker and Rachel Blum, MAGA voters tend to be white, male, and conservative. They make up anywhere from 42 to 80 percent of Republican-leaning voters. "A MAGA Republican is first and foremost a Trump supporter, no matter what he seems to do or say," political scientist James Thurber said.

Delegates show their support for MAGA policies at the 2016 Republican National Convention. Trump defeated sixteen other candidates to win the Republican Party's nomination for president.

WHAT DOES MAGA STAND FOR?

MAGA has become a major political movement, and Donald Trump is its face. MAGA Republicans who line up behind Trump believe in dismantling the government down to its most essential functions. But this isn't the first time that the US government has gone through major upheaval. Slavery was one issue that caused division throughout the country and led to the American Civil War (1861–1865). The Civil Rights Movement of the middle of the twentieth century was another.

MAGA voters are less loyal to the Republican Party and more to Trump as an individual. They see him as a source for truthful information, often believing him

In 2021 Trump proposed a third political party. He later suggested the names Patriot Party or Magadonians.

over friends and family, the media, and religious leaders. Around 75 percent of MAGA supporters said they would be open to breaking away from the two-party system dominated by Democrats and Republicans for a third party that was led by Trump. Almost nine out of ten MAGA voters believe that America's values, traditions, and wealth are under threat. They admire the way Trump responds to those perceived threats.

The economy, immigration, and border security are the top issues for many MAGA voters.

Many MAGA supporters also hold some controversial beliefs. Nearly 90 percent of MAGA voters don't believe Joe Biden's election in 2020 was legitimate. However, voting in the United States has been proven to be secure and accurate. Only 25 percent believed that what happened at the US Capitol on January 6 was an insurrection or a riot. MAGA supporters are also twice as likely as non-MAGA voters to refuse vaccines. But vaccines have been proven to work and are tested for safety and effectiveness. By 2023, nearly 5.6 billion people, or around 72 percent of the world's population, had been vaccinated against COVID-19.

MAGA voters believe that undocumented people entering the US is a major problem for the country. Quickly deporting millions of people who have illegally crossed the border is a priority, despite the potential costs and threats to the economy. Trump promised to sign emergency orders addressing immigration, and he did so on day one of his second term. He immediately declared a national emergency at the southern border where many undocumented people enter the United States and ended some programs that allowed immigrants to come to the country legally. Immigration and Customs Enforcement (ICE) was given more power to arrest people, creating an atmosphere of fear among many born outside the country. Even some US citizens were detained and questioned.

LGBTQIA+ people were one of the only voting demographics that did not shift toward Trump in the 2024 election. Most LGBTQIA+ people see MAGA as a threat to their basic human rights. Trump's campaign alone spent $17 million on ads targeting Kamala Harris, his opponent in the 2024 election, and her support for transgender rights. One of Trump's first acts as president in 2025 was to limit transgender and nonbinary people's rights. Many MAGA voters see people in this group as a threat to family values and traditional gender dynamics. They fear their vision of American life is disappearing.

Around 93 percent of Trump's base says the economy is important to them. Higher unemployment makes people feel like they are being forgotten. This is especially true in rural areas, as technology replaces human workers on farms, in factories, and in mines.

Gun control is another important issue for MAGA supporters. Trump supports allowing more people, including those with criminal records, to arm themselves.

In January 2025, Trump signed an executive order to rename the Gulf of Mexico the Gulf of America. He said the change would honor American greatness.

Tariffs and Trade

The world economy slowed during the COVID-19 pandemic that began in 2019. Increased demand for products combined with limited supplies pushed up prices. President Biden and Congress enacted stimulus payments and other measures to help people through the tough times. But even after the pandemic, prices continued to rise faster than usual. People's savings and paychecks lost value and buying power.

When Trump took office in 2017, he promised to impose tariffs on Mexico, Canada, and China, three of the US's biggest trade partners. Tariffs are taxes a government imposes on goods that are imported from another country. Tariffs can also mean taxes on exported goods. In 2025 Trump doubled down on his plan and imposed tariffs on imported goods from a broad range of countries.

MAGA voters believe that tariffs will help encourage companies to move factories from overseas, where many have moved to take advantage of lower costs, back to the United States and solve many economic problems. However, it is expensive to relocate factories. American workers have more rights and make more money than workers in many other countries. The US also has strong environmental regulations that can raise costs for companies. And tariffs are not paid by other countries. They are paid by the companies that import the goods. Then, they pass those costs on to the customer, so imported goods such as cars, lumber, and fuel go up in price. Many countries responded by imposing tariffs on goods imported from the US and even boycotting US products.

Yard signs are an instant and public way to show support. Small signs, billboards, and even signs on buildings can have an impact on how people in a community vote.

And he took millions of dollars in campaign donations from the National Rifle Association, a group that works to expand gun rights. His support for guns helps him with rural voters who see firearm ownership as part of their way of life.

That connection is why Trump has strongly outperformed his election opponents in rural America. White rural Americans—especially men—who felt forgotten by Washington politicians helped him win in both 2016 and 2024. Many had never voted before. These voters didn't always feel comfortable expressing their feelings publicly. But they found like-minded people online in places like 4chan, Reddit, and X. They shared memes on Facebook that summed up their thoughts. They watched videos on YouTube that validated their feelings. They listened to podcasts such as *The Ben Shapiro Show* and *The Joe Rogan Experience* that welcomed guests who shared their opinions even when many others saw them as controversial. By rejecting mainstream media and career politicians, they would return government to the people and help America to be great again.

Fake News

In 2016 news stories with fake headlines flooded social media. They originated in Macedonia. A group of young people had created clickbait as a moneymaking scheme. The hottest topic at the time? The US presidential election.

In 2018 Trump (*right*) revoked the White House press pass for CNN reporter Jim Acosta (*left*). CNN sued Trump and his staff for violating Acosta's first amendment rights. The pass was restored a few days later.

Misinformation has always been shared on the internet. But in recent years, social media algorithms, bots, targeted advertising, and share buttons have made it easier than ever to spread it—and harder than ever to identify. Leading up to the 2016 election, around one-quarter of all Americans visited a fake news website. Studies show that some people develop false memories after reading fake news. Social media algorithms also place people in echo chambers that only include similar voices. These spaces amplify the beliefs people already have, without offering many other alternative ideas or differing opinions.

In early 2017, Trump told CNN reporter Jim Acosta, "You're fake news." He also began using the phrase on X. Millions of other people—both MAGA and otherwise—began borrowing it as well. Soon, fake news didn't just apply to false information. It could refer to conspiracy theories, human error, or just information people didn't like or agree with. Some people began mistrusting everything they saw from news sites. In a study of forty-six countries, the United States media ranked the lowest in terms of public trust.

REJECTING MAGA

Although MAGA has roots in the Republican Party, not all Republicans are MAGA. Some question Trump's character and fitness for the job of president. Others think MAGA takes conservative principles too far, is too isolationist in a world that depends on American leadership, and isn't a strong defender of democracy.

After losing to Joe Biden in the 2020 presidential election, Trump had continually pressured Vice President Mike Pence to deny the results were valid. As vice president, it was Pence's responsibility to oversee the election certification process. He had no power to stop it. He refused Trump's demands. Pence had been Trump's loyal ally for years, refusing to criticize the president.

Trump's social media post about Mike Pence during the January 6 insurrection was shown during an investigative hearing in 2022. In the post, Trump called out Pence's refusal to overturn the election and said Pence lacked courage.

However, the January 6 riot was a breaking point for Pence. In turn, Trump posted on social media that Pence didn't have the courage to protect the country. As rioters overran the Capitol, some even called to execute Pence.

In June 2023, Pence announced his bid for the 2024 presidential race. However, he dropped out in October. He could not find enough support to launch a full campaign. To many, he was seen as a staunch conservative. But among MAGA supporters, he was seen as a traitor. In 2024 he stepped out of the political spotlight and took a job teaching at a small conservative college. After Trump won reelection, Pence returned to politics, spearheading a group opposing Robert F. Kennedy, Trump's pick for Secretary of Health and Human Services. Pence gave speeches urging Trump to renew and strengthen ties to foreign allies, even meeting with foreign leaders on his own.

Several other Republicans distanced themselves from Trump and his followers. One of the first—and the loudest—was George Conway,

George Conway (*pictured*) and the Lincoln Project endorsed both Joe Biden and Kamala Harris. They also ran campaigns against politicians who supported Trump.

then-husband of Trump's senior counselor, Kellyanne Conway. George Conway was an attorney and activist. He cofounded The Lincoln Project in 2019, a political action committee (PAC) run by moderate conservatives and former Republicans whose goal is to protect democracy from threats they see from Trump and MAGA. The PAC bought ads calling out companies that supported MAGA members of Congress. Other ads targeted conservative voters and pointed out Trump's flaws.

Liz Cheney was another Republican who spoke out against MAGA. Her father was former vice president Dick Cheney, and Wyoming elected her to the US House of Representatives in 2016. They reelected her in 2018 and 2020. Cheney rose to become the third-highest ranking Republican in the House.

At first, Cheney appeared to see eye-to-eye with Trump. She stood with him during his first impeachment in December 2019. Impeachment is a trial against a public official for misconduct or wrongdoing. A House inquiry had found that Trump withheld $400 million in military funding to Ukraine to pressure the country to launch an investigation into Joe Biden. Such an investigation could have swayed the election in Trump's favor. Cheney's lifetime voting record was around 93 percent in support of Trump's ideas. But she also spoke up on issues that were important to her. She praised Dr. Anthony Fauci's treatment of the COVID-19 pandemic when many other Republicans attacked him. Fauci had been the director of the National Institute of Allergy and Infectious Diseases for nearly four decades. MAGA voters criticized Fauci for his policies during the pandemic, including encouraging the use of protective masks, social distancing in public places, and shutting down schools and businesses. Many felt that Fauci's ideas were too heavy-handed and didn't respect individual freedoms.

Trump is the only federal official to have been impeached more than once. His second impeachment was in January 2021. Cheney was one of only ten House Republicans who voted to impeach Trump over his support of the January 6 assault on the Capitol. "There has never been a greater betrayal by a president of the United States of his office and his oath to the Constitution," she said.

Liz Cheney (*front row right*) supported Kamala Harris (*front row middle*) during Harris's presidential campaign in 2024.

MAGA voters expect elected Republican officials and other government workers to show loyalty to Trump and MAGA principles.

MAGA Republicans, led by influential party members including Steve Scalise, Jim Jordan, and Andy Biggs, worked to oust Cheney. In May 2021, the House Republicans voted to remove her as a party leader. They replaced her with Elise Stefanik, a MAGA-endorsed politician. A few months later, the Wyoming GOP Central Committee removed Cheney from the party altogether.

It soon became clear that a key part of the MAGA movement was showing complete loyalty to Trump. Trump's approval can boost a politician to a high office. However, disagreeing with him can ruin a politician's future.

Immigration Issues

Many people describe MAGA as a nativist movement. Nativism is a political ideology that strives to protect the interests of long-term citizens over recent immigrants. When Trump talks about illegal immigrants and undocumented people crossing the US border, MAGA supporters believe that he is not speaking about US citizens and legal immigrants. However, in January 2025 he called to strip naturalized citizens of their rights, and by March he began moving against legal immigrants, tourists, and foreign students studying in the US as well.

MAGA's populism can appeal to people of any ethnic background. Populism attracts people who feel like the elite—in this case career politicians—are not listening to them. Populists stress taking back power for the people. Disenfranchised people who feel like their rights or privileges have been taken away may feel like populism is the answer.

In March 2025, millions of protesters around the United States took to the streets to speak out against Trump's policies, including those that made cuts to programs for education, veteran and human services, the environment, and immigration.

MAGA MOVING

In Trump's 2016 win, the MAGA movement spoke primarily to white, rural voters, especially men without college degrees and those older than 50. His 2024 win looked different. He maintained the same core voting block of white, rural voters. But he also swayed young Black and Latino men more than in the two previous elections, and he won more men from all age groups, including college-educated men. The picture of who MAGA was had changed.

When people voted in 2024, they thought back to Trump's first term and decided they liked what they remembered. Voters thought interest rates and grocery prices were too high in 2024, and Trump promised to lower both. Some Latinos said they were in favor of Trump's tough immigration policies. Some Black voters felt that the Democratic Party made many promises leading up to elections but then failed to follow through. And other new Trump voters—male and female—said they did not think America was ready for a woman president. Even though these new MAGA voters were not a huge chunk of the population, there were enough to sway the election in Trump's favor.

MAGA is part of a right-wing wave that has spread around the globe. There are similar populist movements gaining traction in many countries. Hungary's Prime Minister Viktor Orbán has praised Trump for America First policies. Italy's prime minister Giorgia Meloni has loudly supported Trump and has a somewhat similar nationalist and isolationist vision for her country. Brazil's former president Jair Bolsonaro endorsed Trump and used social media to gain supporters in a similar fashion. He has said he looks forward to seeing how Trump works with social media billionaires Mark Zuckerberg, who controls Meta, and Elon Musk, who owns X. "Social networks decide elections," Bolsonaro said. Bolsonaro, Zuckerberg, and Musk have adopted slogans with nationalist themes similar to Make America Great Again.

Trump understands the power of social media to promote his MAGA agenda. While many MAGA

Former Brazil president Jair Bolsonaro speaks to supporters. Bolsonaro led a populist movement in Brazil and has been called the Trump of the Tropics.

supporters waited in the cold or packed themselves into a crowded sports arena to watch Trump's inauguration, tech billionaires had front-row seats. Zuckerberg and Musk were included on the guest list. Other influential names included Jeff Bezos, the owner of Amazon and the *Washington Post*; Sundar Pichai, leader of Google; TikTok chief executive Shou Zi Chew; Rupert Murdoch, founder of Fox News and owner of several newspapers including the *Wall Street Journal*; Sam Altman, the leader of OpenAI; and Apple chief executive Tim Cook. Podcaster Joe Rogan and social media influencers Jake and Logan Paul were also there.

From left to right: **Mark Zuckerberg; Lauren Sánchez and her husband, Jeff Bezos; Sundar Pichai; and Elon Musk attend Trump's second inauguration in 2025.**

Monetizing MAGA

Red hats aren't the only MAGA merchandise making big bucks. In January 2025, Trump launched a meme coin called $TRUMP. Each digital coin cost around $7 and was said to be part of a limited supply.

Attendees at the 2024 Republican National Convention could purchase official campaign merchandise.

Every time a coin was sold, traders earned a fee. Some investors made more than $10 million. After two weeks, total fees had reached nearly $100 million. The number of available coins had also increased to one billion. The meme coins were a way for Trump to raise money—and accept money from foreign investors. Those who bought the most were granted access to Trump.

Meme coins are not the only thing Trump has marketed to his supporters. Trump Bibles, shoes, commemorative coins, and watches are only a few of the official items that have been offered. In 2023 a song called "Justice For All" was released. It featured Trump and the J6 Prison Choir, a group of people incarcerated for their role in the January 6 riot. The song reached the number one spot on Billboard's Digital Song Sales.

In 2023 the official Trump Store, owned by the Trump Organization, made more than $3 million in sales. The store listed 1,725 different products on Inauguration Day in 2025.

After Trump began his second term, social media began to change. Facebook got rid of their fact-checking feature and lifted restrictions on subjects including immigration and gender. Posters began noticing that without their prior knowledge, they were suddenly following Trump, Vice President J. D. Vance, and even Melania Trump. Right-wing pages and memes flooded their feeds. Elon Musk had already been prioritizing MAGA rhetoric on his X platform. In 2024 he appeared

Senator Patty Murray (*center*) speaks out against Russell Vought, Trump's pick for the Office of Management and Budget. Vought believes the president should have the power to dismantle the federal government and can act without oversight or accountability. Senate Minority Leader Chuck Schumer (*left*) and Senator Jeff Merkley stand behind Murray.

Elon Musk speaks to reporters in the Oval Office in 2025. Working with Trump, Musk hoped to drastically shrink the size of the federal government.

at a Trump rally at New York City's Madison Square Garden. He wore a black MAGA cap and declared himself to be dark MAGA, a term linked to far-right, extreme MAGA groups. Once Trump took office, Musk became the president's right hand, quickly exerting power over much of the federal government despite not being an elected official. Musk and Trump started the Department of Government Efficiency (DOGE) and placed Musk in charge.

DOGE's goal was to decrease the size of the federal government and maximize government efficiency. These are key goals of both the Tea Party and MAGA movements. DOGE began ordering layoffs for thousands of federal workers on February 13, 2025. It canceled billions of dollars in government contracts. It stopped federal funding of foreign aid, climate science and other scientific research, as well as diversity, equity, and inclusion initiatives. Federal judges immediately began blocking and overturning DOGE's decisions. They stated that DOGE was violating the Constitution. Both Trump and Musk called for those judges to be impeached, setting up a legal and Constitutional showdown.

THE FUTURE OF MAGA

When Trump took office in 2025, he immediately promised a MAGA budget bill. The bill would draw from Project 2025, a nine hundred-page blueprint drawn up by The Heritage Foundation, a conservative think tank. Trump tried to distance himself from Project 2025 before the election, but the executive orders he signed in his first days as president matched the document—or MAGA 2.0, as The Heritage Foundation put it—very closely. Many of Trump's staff picks had been involved in creating Project 2025 as well.

Project 2025 had three hundred total objectives. By spring 2025, more than one hundred had been completed, with another sixty in progress. In February 2025, Republicans proposed a budget that would cut $880 billion to Medicaid. The following month, Trump signed an executive order to dismantle the Department of Education. Any words or subjects relating to diversity were removed from White House websites. Trump also began deporting undocumented people, protected immigrants, and even US citizens. He froze or eliminated many federal jobs and rolled back some workplace safety regulations. Many of those programs and changes directly affected MAGA voters.

Some wonder what the future of MAGA holds and if the movement can survive without Trump. After all, Trump was 78 years old when he was sworn in for his second term. Is there a successor standing by to take up the reins? His vice president, J. D. Vance, is the obvious choice. Other contenders, such as Ron DeSantis, Marco Rubio, and Kari Lake, have not proven they have the following and support for the role. "The only person who's been able to win on the MAGA platform is Trump," Alex Stansberry, the vice president of the Arizona State University College Republicans group, said. And for some young Republicans, Trump's brand of MAGA is all they have ever known. Without the face of MAGA, the movement may fall apart.

Many world leaders see MAGA as synonymous with Trump politics as well. In 2025 after Trump announced interest in purchasing Greenland, which is part of Denmark, Aaja Chemnitz, a member of Denmark's Parliament, said, "Greenland is not for sale. It will never be for sale. . . . Greenland is not MAGA. Greenland is not going to be MAGA." In February, a record number of voters in Germany turned out to reject a far-right political party backed by Vance and Musk. And in April and May, Canada and Australia held elections that ended with losses by conservative, Trump-like politicians. Canada's new prime minister, Mark Carney, had even made a point to run on an anti-Trump, anti-MAGA message.

Trump has captured the hope and attention of people around the country. But his biggest challenge is appealing to a wider range of voters to maintain the MAGA movement's momentum after he leaves office. He must convince them that MAGA policies can make America great for them as well. Trump's second term as president will determine if the MAGA movement is a major force in US politics in the future or just another footnote in the country's long political history.

IMPORTANT DATES

1980	Ronald Reagan uses Let's Make America Great Again as a slogan during his presidential campaign.
February 2009	The Tea Party movement is launched.
June 16, 2015	Donald Trump begins his presidential bid, announcing Make America Great Again as his official slogan.
2015	Trump trademarks Make America Great Again.
November 8, 2016	Trump defeats Hillary Clinton and is elected president of the United States.
2017	Trump first uses the term "fake news."
December 18, 2019	Trump is impeached for the first time.
November 7, 2020	Joe Biden wins the presidency.
January 6, 2020	Thousands of MAGA supporters storm the Capitol to protest the certification of the election.
January 13, 2021	Trump is impeached for the second time.

April 2023	The Heritage Foundation publishes Project 2025.
November 5, 2024	Trump is elected to a second presidential term.
January 20, 2025	Trump signs executive orders that closely parallel the wording of Project 2025. He also pardons everyone charged with January 6 crimes.
February 1, 2025	Trump signs an executive order imposing tariffs on imports from China, Mexico, and Canada. All three countries announce they will impose their own tariffs in response.
April 2, 2025	Trump imposes tariffs on more than 50 additional countries.
May 19, 2025	The Supreme Court gives Trump approval to revoke special legal protections for nearly three hundred fifty thousand people who had fled political instability in Venezuela.

SOURCE NOTES

7 WTOP Staff, "'We Need a Change': Trump Supporters Descent on DC to Celebrate Inauguration," wtop.com, January 20, 2025, https://wtop.com/inauguration/2025/01/pomp-and-freezing-temperatures-donald-trumps-inauguration-events-in-dc/

8 Donald Trump, "The Inaugural Address," Whitehouse.gov, January 2025, https://www.whitehouse.gov/remarks/2025/01/the-inaugural-address/

10 Maya Liquigan, "Ceremony Day Live Updates: Crowds Gather at Capital One Arena for Trump's Inauguration," *The Columbia Chronicle*, January 20, 2025, https://columbiachronicle.com/election-2024/ceremony-day-live-updates-crowds-gather-at-capital-one-arena-for-trumps-inauguration/

13 Widmer, Ted, "Draining the Swamp," *The New Yorker*, https://www.newyorker.com/news/news-desk/draining-the-swamp

26 "Donald Trump Shuts Down CNN Reporter: 'You're Fake News'," CNN, January 11, 2017, https://www.youtube.com/watch?v=Vqpzk-qGxMU

19 Jon Greenberg, "What is a MAGA Republican?" Poynter, September 23, 2022, https://www.poynter.org/fact-checking/2022/what-is-a-maga-republican/

30 Robert Draper, "Liz Cheney vs. MAGA," *The New York Times Magazine*, April 22, 2021, https://www.nytimes.com/2021/04/22/magazine/liz-cheney-vs-maga.html

35 Jack Nicas, "How Can Bolsonaro Avoid Prison? Trump, Musk and Zuckerberg, He Says." *The New York Times*, January 16, 2025, "https://www.nytimes.com/2025/01/16/world/americas/jair-bolsonaro-brazil-trump-us.html

40 Erin Burnett Out Front, "Danish Lawmaker Shares her Assessment of How Greenland Feels about Trump," January 7, 2025, https://edition.cnn.com/2025/01/07/world/video/greenland-not-for-sale-denmark-chemnitz-digvid

41 David Siders, "'I Think We're in Trouble': Is There a Future for MAGA After Trump?" *Politico*, November 4, 2024, https://www.politico.com/news/magazine/2024/11/04/maga-trump-2024-elections-00185283

SELECTED BIBLIOGRAPHY

Blake, Aaron, "7 Ways MAGA Republicans Differ From Other Republicans," *The Washington Post*, August 22, 2023, https://www.washingtonpost.com/politics/2023/08/22/maga-republicans-analysis/

Creel, Nicholas, "Why MAGA Without Trump Could Deliver Landslides to Republicans," *Newsweek*, July 22, 2022, https://www.newsweek.com/why-maga-without-trump-could-deliver-landslides-republicans-opinion-1726493

Fandos, Nicholas, and Catie Edmonson, "In Turning on Liz Cheney, G.O.P. Bows to Trump's Election Lies," *The New York Times*, May 12, 2021, https://www.nytimes.com/2021/05/05/us/politics/liz-cheney-elise-stefanik.html

Garcia, Feliks, "White Men Radicalized Online Were Amongst the 'Silent Majority' Who Chose Donald Trump," *The Independent*, November 14, 2016, https://www.the-independent.com/news/world/americas/us-politics/donald-trump-white-men-online-radicalization-reddit-twitter-alt-right-latest-a7417296.html

Greenblatt, Alan, "For Tea Party, Shutdown Is Worth The Pain," *NPR*, October 13, 2013, https://www.npr.org/sections/itsallpolitics/2013/10/03/228832618/for-tea-party-shutdown-is-worth-the-pain

Jerry, Claire, "A Brief History of Presidential Inaugural Speeches, From George Washington to Today," *Smithsonian Institute*, January 14, 2025, https://www.si.edu/stories/brief-history-presidential-inaugural-speeches

Malik, Nesrine, "Trump 2.0 Is Exposing American Exceptionalism for What It Is—And Has Always Been," The Guardian, February 3, 2025, https://www.theguardian.com/commentisfree/2025/feb/03/donald-trump-american-exceptionalism-guantanamo-bay-imperialism-billionaires

Preskey, Natasha, "Influencers, Tech Bros, MMA Fighters: Trump's Inauguration Guests," *BBC*, January 20, 2025, https://www.bbc.com/news/articles/cgkjgmkn10ko

Quinn, Melissa, "6 Takeaways From Trump's Inaugural Address," *CBS News*, January 21, 2025, https://www.cbsnews.com/news/6-takeaways-from-trumps-inaugural-address/

Wren, Adam, and Sophia Cai, "Trump Takes Victory Lap, Thrills MAGA Crowd at Pre-Inauguration Rally," *Politico*, January 19, 2025, https://www.politico.com/news/2025/01/19/trump-victory-rally-inauguration-00199211

LEARN MORE

Britannica Kids: Donald Trump
https://kids.britannica.com/kids/article/Donald-Trump/628383

The Constitution for Kids
https://www.usconstitution.net/constkids4-html/

Doeden, Matt. *J. D. Vance: From Rural America to the White House.* Lerner Publications, 2025.

History, Art & Archives: United States House of Representatives Student Guides https://history.house.gov/Education/Primary-Sources/Students-Guide/SG/

Leed, Percy. *Donald Trump: Unprecedented Politician.* Lerner Publications, 2025.

Rodriguez, Ann Gaines. *Donald Trump: Our 45th and 47th President.* The Child's World, 2025.

INDEX

PHOTO ACKNOWLEDGMENTS

Image credits: Spencer Platt/Getty Images, p. 2; codyphotography/iStock/Getty Images, p. 6; Kenny Holston-Pool/Getty Images, p. 6; Rena Schild/Shutterstock, p. 8, 16, 24, 26, 32, 36 (background); CHARLY TRIBALLEAU/AFP/Getty Images, p. 9; MPI/Archive Photos/Getty Images, p. 11; Richard Ellis/Getty Images, p. 13; Joshua Lott/Getty Images, p. 14; Joe Raedle/Getty Images, p. 16; Siripak Pason/iStock/Getty Images, p. 16, 24, 26, 32, 36 (background); Bettmann/Getty Images, p. 17; ROBYN BECK/AFP/Getty Images, p. 19; LOGAN CYRUS/AFP/Getty Images, p. 20; Will Waldron/Albany Times Union/Hearst Newspapers/Getty Images, p. 21; Alex Wong/Getty Images, p. 23; Scott Olson/Getty Images, p. 25; MANDEL NGAN/AFP/Getty Images, p. 26; MANDEL NGAN/AFP/Getty Images, p. 27; Sara Stathas/The Washington Post/Getty Images, p. 28; Sarah Rice/Getty Images, p. 30; Jeffery Edwards/Shutterstock, p. 31; Ringo Chiu/Shutterstock, p. 32; MAURO PIMENTEL/AFP/Getty Images, p. 34; Julia Demaree Nikhinson/Pool/Getty Images, p. 35; Anna Moneymaker/Getty Images, p. 36; Chip Somodevilla/Getty Images, p. 37; Andrew Harnik/Getty Images, p. 38

Cover image: Aaron of L.A. Photography/Shutterstock